ILLINOIS WOMEN

75 YEARS OF THE RIGHT TO VOTE

CONTRIBUTORS

HOW THEY WON THE VOTE, *by Kathy Owen Sorensen and Mark W. Sorensen*

CIVIL WAR: THE ROOTS OF A WOMEN'S MOVEMENT, *by Janice Rosenberg*

WOMEN'S HIGHER LEARNING, *by Janice Rosenberg*

CLUBWOMEN ADD THEIR STRENGTH, *by Mary Jean Houde*

THE ALPHA SUFFRAGE CLUB, *by Wanda A. Hendricks*

MEN WHO FOUGHT FOR WOMAN SUFFRAGE, *by Sandra S. Harmon*

WOMEN'S WORK AT THE COLUMBIAN EXPO, *Tonje Kilen*

BIOGRAPHIES BY: *Janice Rosenberg, Richard Seidel, Monica Buckley and Tonje Kilen.*

SITE LISTINGS BY: *Janice Rosenberg, Mary Ann Johnson, Richard Seidel.*

COPY EDITORS: *Fran Buckley and Elizabeth Owens-Schiele*

PROJECT MANAGER, *Monica Buckley*

SPONSORSHIP DEVELOPMENT, *Ida Bialik*

CONSULTANTS, *Mary Todd and Sharon Alter*

ART DIRECTOR, *Cherene Olson*

FILM *BY* LAKE SHORE IMAGING, INC.

PRINTED *BY* SERVICE WEB OFFSET CO.

COVER *PHOTO SUPPLIED BY* CHICAGO HISTORICAL SOCIETY

Performance Media
CHICAGO SUN-TIMES FEATURES, INC.

This publication was produced by Performance Media, in cooperation with
Governor Edgar's Commission for the Celebration of the Seventy-Fifth Anniversary of the Nineteenth Amendment.

Chicago Sun-Times Features, Inc.
401 N. Wabash Ave., Suite 532A
Chicago, Illinois 60611

ISBN Paperback: 1-888682-02-7

*Photographs throughout this publication were supplied by: Illinois State Historical Library,
Chicago Historical Society, University of Illinois at Chicago Historical Library, Illinois State University Daily Vidette,
Wilmette Historical Museum, Peoria Historical Society, Peoria Women's Club, Illinois Labor History Society,
Cairo Public Library, Bentley Historical Library, The Dana Thomas House–Illinois Historic Preservation Agency,
Illinois State Archives, Quincy and Adams Historical Society, Alimay Kendrick, Eric Futran Photography,
The Scholl College of Podiatric Medicine, Southern Illinois University Photocommunications, Sandra S. Harmon,
McHenry County Historical Society, Illinois State University Foundation, Joseph Smith Historic Center,
Todd Rosenberg, The Woodson Branch of the Chicago Public Library, The Frances E. Willard Memorial Library,
Bradley University Cullom–Davis Library, Ned's Photo–Scenics, Galesburg Public Library,
Illinois Secretary of State, Bryn Mawr College Libraries and Jane Addams Hull–House.*

REMEMBER,
GINGER ROGERS
DID EVERYTHING
FRED ASTAIRE
DID,
BUT SHE
DID IT
BACKWARDS
AND IN
HIGH HEELS.

– Faith Whittlesey

TABLE OF CONTENTS

"Part of reaching success as an entrepreneur is knowing the tools to help get you there."
— *Margaret Smith, President, NAWBO*

When Margaret Smith left an established law firm in 1987 to start her own business, she had one goal in mind. She wanted to use her entrepreneurial spirit and thorough knowledge of law to aid other small business owners. "I started what I considered to be the law firm of the future," she says. "By focusing on small and family-run organizations, I was ahead of the trend."

She was also ahead of the trend in technology. "From the day Smith Law Offices opened I was determined to keep my practice and my people up-to-date with the latest technology," Margaret says. "At a time when other firms were shying away from giving their lawyers computers, I made sure we always had one at our fingertips. It was a revolutionary concept. I wanted the tools to do the job better and IBM was there to help."

Recently Margaret's son became a partner in the firm, making it a family run business like many of her clients. Together they use IBM's 586 Pentium computer to keep business on track. An IBM Thinkpad also helps Margaret keep up with her busy schedule—including her role as President of the National Association of Women Business Owners.

IBM is proud to salute and support Margaret Smith and the many women like her. In today's changing business world, we know that continued success is sure to be the final verdict.

Jane Addams in a Suffrage Parade, passing the Art Institute of Chicago, 1910.

HOW THEY WON THE VOTE

BY KATHY OWEN SORENSEN
& MARK W. SORENSEN

Throughout the nineteenth century, most American women could not vote or hold office. When Illinois entered the Union in 1818, its constitution expressly gave the vote only to "white, male inhabitants above the age of twenty-one years." The other twenty states had similar restrictions. New Jersey women could vote in 1776, but the right was taken away from them in 1807.

By mid-century, some women who had been active in the fight to abolish slavery began to feel that it was not only slaves who were oppressed, but also women. Early suffragist Elizabeth Cady Stanton wrote: "The history of mankind is a history of repeated injuries...on the part of man toward women; having (as its) object an absolute tyranny over women."

Illinois's second constitution, adopted in 1848, allowed men to vote for a greater number of officials than had the previous constitution, but it still excluded women from voting. That same year, at a convention held in Seneca Falls, New York, three hundred women and men came together to discuss women's rights. At this meeting, the group issued twelve declarations. The only one to pass *without* unanimous approval stated: "It is the duty of the women of this country to secure to themselves their sacred right to the elective franchise." Yet, with this declaration—which voiced what was a radical idea at the time—the woman suffrage movement in the United States began.

Two Elephants carry the "Suffrage Plank" at the 1916 Republican Party National Convention in Chicago.

The movement gathered momentum slowly over the next few years. Until the Civil War began in 1861, most women activists put their energy into the fight to abolish slavery. With the beginning of hostilities, women abolitionists turned their attention to the war effort. In Illinois, Mary A. Livermore, Jane C. Hoge, and other women helped establish the U.S. Army Sanitary Commission, a relief agency and forerunner of the Red Cross, which provided supplies to soldiers and operated battlefield hospitals.

Participation in the abolitionist movement and the Civil War gave many women confidence and organizational skills. When the war ended in 1865, these same women felt that their essential role in it had earned them the right to fuller participation in government. However, in 1868, the Fourteenth Amendment was added to the U.S. Constitution, introducing for the first time language that

ALL ACROSS EUROPE, AS THE NEW DAY ARRIVES, SO DO WE.

Bodiam Castle, Sussex, England.

It happens in London, Paris and Frankfurt just as

the city starts to stir. In Zurich, Manchester and Milan. In Stockholm,

Glasgow, Birmingham, Brussels and Madrid.

American arrives as each new day begins.

With more service from Chicago to Europe than any other U.S. airline.

For flight reservations or information about our affordable Fly AAway Vacations® packages,

call your Travel Agent or American at **1-800-624-6262.**

AmericanAirlines®
Something special to Europe.®

FRANCE ITALY SWEDEN SPAIN BELGIUM SWITZERLAND SCOTLAND ENGLAND GERMANY

Fly AAway Vacations is a registered trademark of American Airlines, Inc.

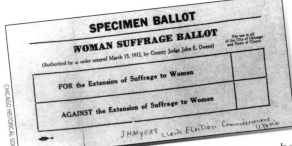

specifically described voters as "male." This meant that in order for all American women to have the right to vote secured by federal law, a new amendment would have to be adopted.

In 1870, the Fifteenth Amendment was ratified, declaring that the right to vote could not be denied due to race, color, or prior servitude. Women, however, were still deprived of this right. Frustrated at being blocked at the federal level, many suffragists began to concentrate on obtaining the vote one state at a time.

In Illinois, on February 12, 1869, Susan B. Anthony and Elizabeth Cady Stanton came to Chicago to discuss women's rights, and the Illinois Woman Suffrage Association (IWSA) was formed with Mary Livermore as its president. In 1870, Illinois was drafting its third constitution. Women from the IWSA attended the constitutional convention in Springfield to encourage legislators to include women's voting rights.

Petitions containing 1,600 signatures in favor of woman suffrage were countered by antisuffrage petitions with 1,381 signatures. Frances Willard, soon to be the first Dean of Women at Northwestern University, declared: "The idea that boys of twenty-

Five thousand women marched in the rain to the Republican Party Convention hall in 1916 to demand a Woman Suffrage plank in the party platform.

one are fit to make laws for their mothers, is an insult to everyone." In May 1870, however, a new state constitution was adopted that provided suffrage for African American males—but not for women.

Through legislation passed in 1891, Illinois women won the right to vote in elections for school officials throughout the state. Subsequent Illinois Supreme Court cases allowed women to cast ballots for, and serve as, University of Illinois trustees. In 1894, Chicago social welfare leader Lucy Flower ran for trustee and received more votes than anyone running for state office that year. She was the first woman elected by voters statewide.

Many suffragists continued to resent the fact that African American men and many recently arrived immigrant men could vote while women remained deprived of this right. Under the leadership of Evanston attorney Catharine Waugh McCulloch, the state suffrage association, renamed the Illinois Equal Suffrage Association (IESA), kept pressure on the General Assembly for the next twenty years. This resulted in the introduction of a suffrage bill every two years, but none passed.

A 1915 Harper's Weekly cover illustration.

Few men were convinced that women should get the vote. A man claiming to be a representative of the "Man Suffrage Association" wrote his senator, claiming that "every socialist, anarchist and Bolshevist" was for woman suffrage. One man exclaimed that women had done nothing to deserve the vote, that they were merely "the passive and often unwilling and hostile instruments by which humanity is created."

Because of suffragists' close ties to the temperance movement, the liquor lobby was steadfastly opposed to giving women the vote. When a ballot asking whether or not women should be given the vote was included in the 1912 Chicago primary election, the proposition was defeated 135,410 to 71,354.

That same year, the IESA changed its tactics. Newly elected president Grace Wilbur Trout abandoned McCulloch's confrontational style. She made sure a local organization was started in every senatorial district. One of her assistants, Glencoe suffrage leader Elizabeth Knox Booth, studied the legislators' records and personal interests in order to better persuade them to support woman suffrage. Ruth Hanna McCormick, who later became a U.S. congresswoman from Illinois, stayed in touch with the Springfield newspaper correspondents. This helped to ensure positive reports on suffrage. Antoinette Funk, a lawyer from Chicago, persuaded some opponents, if not to vote for suffrage, at least to refrain from fighting passage of the bill.

A flyer for the Woman's Party Convention in 1916.

During the 1913 session of the General Assembly, a bill was once again introduced that would allow women to vote for presidential electors as well as some local officials. With the help of first-term Speaker of the House William McKinley, the bill was given to a favorable committee. McKinley told Trout that he would bring it up for a final vote only if he were convinced there was support for the bill. Trout opened the floodgates of her network, and while McKinley was in Chicago over the weekend, he received a phone call every fifteen minutes, day and night. On his return to Springfield he found a deluge of telegrams and letters from all over the state.

The bill passed the Senate first, and was brought up for a House vote on June 11, 1913. Trout and her troops counted heads and actually visited residences of absent pro-suffrage representatives to bring them to vote. Trout herself guarded the door to the House chambers and urged members in favor of the bill not to leave before voting. She also tried to prevent "anti" lobbyists from being allowed onto the floor illegally. With all twenty-five first-term Progressives and three Socialist Party members voting for it, the bill passed 83–58 and was signed into law by Governor Edward F. Dunne.

Illinois women could now vote for president and for all local offices except those specifically named in the Illinois Constitution. Women still had to use separate ballots and ballot boxes. But, by virtue of the new law, Illinois became the first state east of the Mississippi River to grant women the right to vote in presidential elections.

The passage of the Municipal Voting Act was a landmark event in the national suffrage movement. Suffrage leader Carrie Chapman Catt wrote: "The effect of this victory upon the nation was astounding. When the first Illinois election took place in April (1914), the press carried the headlines that 250,000 women had voted in Chicago. Illinois, with its large electoral vote of twenty-nine, proved the turning point beyond which politicians at last got a clear view of the fact that women were gaining genuine political power."

On March 3, 1913, more than 5,000 suffragists paraded in Washington, D.C. Once the parade started down Pennsylvania Avenue, the crowd of spectators became abusive and closed in on the marchers. With local police doing little to keep control, the cavalry was called in. More than 100 women were hospitalized. Public sympathy aroused by the incident caused many suffragists to conclude that public protests would be the quickest route to universal suffrage.

By the end of 1914, women had won the right to vote for president in twelve states. In 1915, Carrie Chapman Catt for the second time assumed the presidency of the National American Woman Suffrage Association. Her campaign, called the Winning Plan, encouraged work at the state level, but made it clear that a federal amendment was the ultimate goal.

In June 1916, the Republican Party National Convention was held in Chicago. In a tremendous rainstorm, five thousand women marched to the convention hall to demand a woman suffrage plank in the party platform. Their efforts were rewarded by presidential candidate Charles Evans Hughes's endorsement of the proposed amendment to the U.S. Constitution.

Over the next few years, the public would become increasingly aware of the suffragists' efforts. During World War I, Alice Paul led the more militant women in the national movement in a protest, picketing the White House. The women objected to U.S. involvement in the fight for democracy abroad, claiming that democratic principles were not being upheld at home. Over a five-month period beginning in July 1917, 168 women were imprisoned for "disrupting traffic." In response to public outcry over the mistreatment of the imprisoned suffragists, President Wilson ordered

A Woman Suffrage float in Chicago's July 4th parade, 1910.

Grace Wilbur Trout at the wheel of a Woman Suffrage car. Suffrage leaders spoke from these vehicles as they travelled through communities across the state.

their unconditional release. Finally, in early 1918, the previously resistant president publicly stated his support for a woman suffrage amendment. It was not until September of that year, however, that he addressed the Senate with an argument in its favor.

In June 1919, Congress finally passed the Susan B. Anthony Amendment. First proposed by Anthony in 1878, it stated simply: "The right of citizens of the United States to vote shall not be denied or abridged by the United States or by any state on account of sex." The amendment then went to the states for ratification. On June 10, 1919, Illinois became the first state to ratify it. Twelve months later, thirty-six states had approved it, and on August 26, 1920, the Nineteenth Amendment was officially declared part of the U.S. Constitution.

Perhaps Catt summarized the history of the seventy-two-year-long suffrage struggle best when she wrote: "Hundreds of women gave the accumulated possibilities of an entire lifetime...hundreds of thousands gave constant interest, and such aid as they could...Young suffragists who helped forge the last links of that chain were not born when it began. Old suffragists who forged the first links were dead when it ended."

In honoring the contributions of those who came before them, the League of Women Voters and other women's organizations conducted commemorative events throughout 1995 to emphasize the significance of the suffrage movement in American history and the contributions of women in politics today.

Strength, Wisdom and Leadership

Young Woman Bathing Her Feet in a Brook, Camille Pissarro, 1895

Through our customers, employees and board of directors, the influence

of women is reflected in everything we do at

Sara Lee Corporation. We celebrate your achievements and thank you

for your strength, wisdom and leadership.

SARA LEE CORPORATION

Hanes Hanes Her Way L'eggs Bali Champion Playtex Coach Kiwi Jimmy Dean Hillshire Farm Ball Park Douwe Egberts Sara Lee

ILLINOIS TIMELINE

1812 *May 20*: Illinois becomes a territory, with suffrage for all white males over 21 who pay taxes and have lived in the territory over a year.

1818 Illinois enters the Union. Its constitution gives the vote to "white male inhabitants above the age of twenty-one years."

1844 Illinois women form the first anti-slavery society. The abolitionist cause begins to function as a training ground for the women's rights movement.

1848 Illinois's second constitution is drafted, still excluding women from voting.

1855 First Suffrage meeting is held in Earlville at the home of Susan Hoxie Richardson, a cousin of national suffrage leader Susan B. Anthony.

1861 *February 21*: Act is passed, allowing married women to own and sell their own property.

1869 Myra Bradwell is refused admission to the Illinois Bar. She appeals to the United States Supreme Court.

February 11-12: First Midwest Suffrage Convention is held during which the Illinois Woman Suffrage Association is formed and Illinois suffragist Mary Livermore is named president.

March 24: Act is passed stating, "a married woman shall be entitled to receive, use and possess her own earnings."

1870 Illinois Woman Suffrage Association holds its first annual convention in the state capitol of Springfield to coincide with the Illinois state constitutional convention.

May: A third constitution is drafted, expanding the franchise to African American males, but not to women.

1872 *March 22*: Act is passed prohibiting discrimination in employment because of sex. This was the first law in the country prohibiting this kind of discrimination.

1873 Statute is passed recognizing women's eligibility to hold school office.

1874 Ten women in Illinois are elected County Superintendents of Schools.

1889 *September 18*: Hull–House, one of the earliest settlement houses in the United States, is founded by Jane Addams and Ellen Gates Starr to serve poor immigrant families on Chicago's West Side.

1891 *April 6*: Ellen Martin votes in Lombard Municipal election, having discovered the town charter's description of voters as "citizens." The charter was swiftly changed.

June 19: Women are granted the right to vote in school board elections.

1892 *March 22*: Myra Bradwell, Alta Hulett, Ada Kepley and others get a bill passed that bars discrimination in employment.

1893 *May 1-October 30*: World's Columbian Exposition, held on Chicago's South Side, commemorates the 400th anniversary of Columbus's discovery of America.

1897 Caroline Corbin forms the Illinois Association Opposed to the Extension of Suffrage to Women.

1913 *June 26*: The General Assembly grants women the right to vote in presidential elections, making Illinois the first state east of the Mississippi to do so.

1916 *June 7-10*: The Republican national convention in Chicago nominates Charles E. Hughes for president. Five thousand women march in the rain demanding a suffrage plank in the party platform.

1923 Illinois Equal Rights Bill, which would guarantee legal equality for women, is introduced into the Illinois General Assembly. Illinois National Woman's Party legislative chairperson Susan Lawrence Dana leads a vigorous campaign, but the bill fails in June.

1963 Illinois Commission on the Status of Women is established. On March 31, 1985, it was absorbed into the Citizens Assembly, and in 1995, no funds were allocated for the Citizen's Assembly.

1968 *November 28-30*: Over 200 women from 37 states and Canada hold the first women's liberation conference in Chicago, bringing a national character to the radical women's movement.

1970 *December 15*: The new 1970 Illinois Constitution in Article I, Section 18 provides that equal protection of the laws shall not be denied or abridged on account of sex by the state or other governmental units.

1972 Equal Rights Amendment to the U. S. Constitution is considered in Illinois legislature. Although it receives a majority in both houses, it fails to get the controversial three–fifths majority required by the Illinois Constitution.

1982 Illinois Domestic Violence Act is passed, making domestic violence a crime. In 1986, the law is expanded to allow women to get orders of protection.

1984 Illinois Criminal Sexual Assault Act is passed, providing more protection for women testifying in rape cases.

1995 *April 12*: Home Occupation Ordinance is passed in Chicago after years of effort on the part of women's groups, legalizing the estimated 280,000 Chicago home–based businesses, a large number of which are owned by women.

1776 New Jersey legislation grants women the vote in its state constitution.

1807 New Jersey legislators rewrite constitution, denying women the vote.

1848 *July 19-20: Seneca Falls, NY*—First convention to discuss women's rights is led by Lucretia Mott, Elizabeth Cady Stanton and others. The "Declaration of Sentiments and Resolutions" states the program of the women's rights movement.

1850 *October 23-24*: First National Women's Rights Convention is held in Worchester, MA. The convention was planned by early activists Lucy Stone, Lucretia Mott and Abby Kelley.

1866 *May 1*: American Equal Rights Association is formed with Lucretia Mott as president. Members pledge to work for equal suffrage for both women and African-American.

1868 The Fourteenth Amendment to the U. S. Constitution is ratified, using for the first time the word "male" to define a citizen.

1869 *May*: The National Woman Suffrage Association is founded by Susan B. Anthony and Elizabeth Cady Stanton to achieve the vote through a Congressional amendment, while also addressing other women's rights issues.

November 18: The American Woman Suffrage Association is formed by Lucy Stone, Henry Blackwell and other more conservative activists to work on amending individual state constitutions.

1871 *January 11*: Victoria Woodhull addresses the U. S. House Judiciary Committee, arguing women's right to vote under the Fourteenth Amendment.

The Anti-Suffrage Party is founded by the wives of prominent men, such as Civil War generals.

1872 Susan B. Anthony is arrested in New York with 15 other women for casting a ballot. She is tried and fined $100, but she refuses to pay.

1890 The American Woman Suffrage Association and the National Woman Suffrage Association merge, becoming the National American Woman Suffrage Association (NAWSA), pledged to state-by-state campaigns for suffrage.

July 23: Wyoming is admitted to the Union. It is the first state since New Jersey (1776–1807) to grant women full enfranchisement.

1913 The Congressional Union is formed by Alice Paul and Lucy Burns as an auxiliary of the National American Woman Suffrage Association, for the exclusive purpose of securing passage of a federal amendment.

1913 *May 10*: The largest suffrage parade to date is held in New York City. Five thousand suffragists, including 500 men, march down Fifth Avenue past 500,000 onlookers.

1916 *August*: National American Woman Suffrage Association's state chapters endorse NAWSA President Carrie Chapman Catt's "Winning Plan," —a unified campaign to get a federal amendment through Congress and ratified by the states.

1917 *January 10*: The National Woman's Party (NWP), headed by Alice Paul, pickets in front of the White House.

1919 *May 21*: The U. S. House of Representatives passes the federal woman suffrage amendment 304 to 89, 42 votes over the required two–thirds majority.

June 4: The U. S. Senate passes the Nineteenth Amendment with just two votes to spare, 56 to 25. It is then sent to the states for ratification.

1920 *February 14*: The League of Women Voters is founded at the Victory Convention of the National American Woman Suffrage Association in Chicago.

August 18: Tennessee becomes the thirty–sixth state to ratify the Suffrage Amendment. A young state legislator casts the deciding vote after being admonished to do so by his mother.

August 26: The Nineteenth Amendment is quietly signed into law by U. S. Secretary of State Bainbridge Colby, granting women the right to vote.

1961 President John F. Kennedy establishes the President's Commission on the Status of Women, the first commission to formally address "women's issues."

1963 Equal Pay Act is passed, requiring equal pay for men and women with the same jobs.

1964 Civil Rights Act is passed, including Title VII, the equal employment opportunities section banning sex discrimination.

1966 *June 28*: Twenty–eight women form the National Organization of Women (NOW) at the National Conference of State Commissions on the Status of Women in Washington, D.C.

1972 *March 22*: Equal Rights Amendment is passed from U. S. Senate to states for ratification. A decade of campaigning for equal rights begins.

1973 Roe v. Wade: Supreme Court decision recognizes abortion as a constitutional right, making it legal in all states.

1977 *November*: The first national meeting for women's rights since the Seneca Falls convention in 1848 is held at the United Nations meeting in Houston, Texas.

1982 Equal Rights Amendment is not ratified.

1992 Family Leave Act is passed, requiring businesses to allow employees a leave of absence after the birth or adoption of a child.

*Chicago Teachers'
Federation leader
Margaret A. Haley
(standing right) in a
Suffrage Parade.*

THE WOMEN WHO MADE IT HAPPEN

Illinois has been home to a great number of our country's women of leadership. Ida B. Wells, Frances Willard and Jane Addams all achieved national acclaim for their social activism, and we proudly tell their stories here.

But many of the state's most influential women, particularly those whose contribution was local in nature, are virtually unknown to the layperson. Myra Bradwell, for example, who published the influential legal journal, *Chicago Legal News*, after her application to the Illinois bar was refused on account of her sex in 1869, wrote much of the women's rights legislation of the 1870s and 1880s.

Mary Livermore, who prior to the Civil War believed that women should not have the right to vote, was co-director and master fund raiser of the Chicago branch of the U.S. Sanitary Commission, which aided the war effort in the North. After the war, Livermore declared that little of the country's pressing business was getting done, and that if this were to be rectified, women must be able to vote. She established the Illinois Woman Suffrage Association in 1869.

With the following biographical sketches, arranged in alphabetical order by last name and interspersed with illuminating historical essays, the reader will meet Illinois women who made a difference. Though we could not list them all, we present these stories as a contribution to the growing effort to write women back into history.

SADIE LEWIS ADAMS (DATES UNKNOWN)

Sadie Lewis Adams

Clubwoman and public servant Sadie Lewis Adams worked for many Chicago associations including the Gaudeamus Charity Club, the Chicago Urban League, Provident Hospital and the Illinois Home and Aid Society. She served as president and secretary of the Alpha Suffrage Club. As the club's delegate she was Illinois's only representative at the 1916 National Equal Rights League meeting in Washington. In 1922, she was the only African American delegate from Illinois to attend the Women Voters' Convention of the Pan–American Congress National League.

JANE ADDAMS

Jane Addams was a latecomer to the struggle for woman suffrage. She had advocated the vote for women as early as 1897, but even then her efforts were strongest in the broader movement of women's rights, especially concerning women's role in the family and the work place. She joined the National American Woman Suffrage Association (NAWSA) in 1906 and began to devote more of her time to speaking and writing for the suffrage cause. Traveling across the nation, she lectured on campuses and before woman's clubs, arguing persuasively that women should take a more prominent role in government and society by applying their traditional housekeeping skills to "civic housekeeping."

In 1911, Addams became a NAWSA vice president, and used the position to launch a more aggressive campaign in Illinois. She went to Springfield with a trainload of

Jane Addams

three hundred women supporters. They testified before legislative committees, approached legislators in the corridors of the Capitol, and met with them in their offices, but to no avail.

When Theodore Roosevelt formed the Progressive Party in 1912, Addams seconded his nomination and threw herself into the campaign with enthusiasm. The Progressive Party's platform included social reform issues, including woman suffrage. Addams served on party committees, wrote in progressive journals, and spoke in cities and towns throughout the country. She continued to support the Progressive Party for a while after it lost the 1912

election, but shifted her support to Woodrow Wilson in 1916, believing he would heed her call to support social reform in America.

In 1913, Addams attended the Woman's International Suffrage Association convention in Budapest. She continued to travel extensively on behalf of woman suffrage. Although her faith in the suffrage movement never wavered, she began to speak out increasingly on peace issues after the outbreak of World War I. She served as chair of the Woman's Peace Party in 1915, and in that same year she became a delegate to the International Congress of Women. A member of its executive committee, she was invited to chair the conference as a delegate from the largest neutral country.

Despite criticism for her pacifism during World War I, a commitment to the peace movement consumed Addams's energies for the rest of her life, and she received the Nobel Peace Prize in 1931. She died in Chicago on May 21, 1935.

CIVIL WAR: THE ROOTS OF A WOMEN'S MOVEMENT

Events foreshadowing the American Civil War (1861–1865) and the responsibilities women took on during that war sparked the creation of a national woman suffrage movement in the United States. From the 1830s through the 1850s, particularly in the North, abolitionism and feminism were almost inseparable in the minds of many women. Those who worked for the antislavery cause learned how to speak in public and how to demand civil rights for others, and they began to realize the extent of discrimination against women.

Prior to the Civil War, women worked in a variety of humanitarian and philanthropic organizations. For example, in 1844 the Female Anti-Slavery Society was formed by the women of Illinois. When the war began, these women were well suited to taking on the large-scale work of the U. S. Sanitary Commission. Across the Midwest, they nursed soldiers and raised funds for rations and hospital supplies.

Immediately following the war, women who had worked in the Sanitary Commission began systematically applying their organizational skills and resources to the local women's rights movement.

—*Janice Rosenberg*

Ella G. Berry (date unknown–1939)

Chicagoan Ella G. Berry was active in church work and women's club activity. Her interest in suffrage led her to the field of politics. She was the state organizer of the Hughes Colored Women's Clubs for the National Republican Headquarters in 1919 and an investigator for the Commission on Race Relations. Appointed in 1922 as a Home Visitor charged with assessing the needs of poor families, Ella G. Berry became the first African American to hold a position in the Department of Public Welfare.

Ella G. Berry

Mary Ann Ball Bickerdyke (1817–1901)

When the Civil War began, Mary Ann Ball Bickerdyke was a widow living in Galesburg with her two sons. In June 1861, she volunteered to deliver medical relief funds to a military hospital in Cairo, Illinois. Shocked by the terrible conditions in the hospital, she stayed for nine months. She did laundry, cooked meals, and nursed sick and wounded men.

Bickerdyke quickly became famous among soldiers as "Mother Bickerdyke." Over the next four years, she cared for the men in Union army field hospitals, on U.S. Sanitary Commission hospital ships, and on battlefields. In 1863, at the cold and rainy battle of Lookout Mountain in Tennessee, she was the only woman nursing hundreds of wounded Union soldiers.

Not everyone welcomed her, but Bickerdyke took criticism in stride. According to legend, when a surgeon asked on whose authority she acted, she replied, "On the authority of Lord God Almighty; have you anything that outranks that?"

Generals Grant and Sherman valued Bickerdyke's work. When the war ended, she was given an honored place in the Washington, D.C., victory parade of May 24, 1865. In 1886, in recognition of her war work, the U.S. Congress gave her a pension of $25 a month. She died in Bunker Hill, Kansas, on November 8, 1901.

Mary Ann Ball Bickerdyke

LOUISE DE KOVEN BOWEN (1859–1953)

Louise de Koven Bowen was attracted to the struggle for women's right to vote by the example of British suffrage agitators who had chained themselves to an iron fence in a London park and swallowed the keys so that police had to saw through the chains to carry them away. Bowen spoke at a Hull-House meeting, expressing

Louise de Koven Bowen

her respect for these women and declaring that she intended to work for suffrage in this country. Bowen noticed her husband's astonishment as he listened in the audience.

After meeting Jane Addams in 1893, Bowen became involved in the work of Hull-House. One of its principal benefactors, she served as longtime trustee, treasurer, and president. Bowen provided funding for Bowen Hall and the Boys' Club Building, and purchased the Joseph T. Bowen Country Club in Waukegan as a memorial to her husband. This club served as the Hull-House summer camp.

Bowen attended almost every suffrage convention with Addams, served as an officer in several national, state and local organizations, and spoke in support of suffrage in auditoriums and churches around the country. In 1923, three years after the ratification of the Nineteenth Amendment, she considered seeking the Republican candidacy for mayor of Chicago. During the 1920s and thereafter, she lamented that women were not exercising their vote in large enough numbers and that not enough women were candidates or elected officials.

Despite her close friendship with Addams, Bowen disapproved of Addams's pacifism during World War I, when Bowen became chair of the Illinois division of the Women's Council of Defense. She later acted as the American delegate to the Pan American Conference on Women in 1923 and served for many years as president of the Juvenile Protective Association. Following Addams's death in 1935, Bowen took an even stronger leadership role at Hull-House.

WOMEN'S HIGHER LEARNING

Secondary schools for women were established in the United States during the first half of the nineteenth century. Approximately two hundred female seminaries for young women were scattered across the country by the beginning of the Civil War. Unlike the New England "finishing schools," or "dame schools," of the 1700s, seminaries offered serious academic study for women.

In Illinois, twenty-seven seminaries for girls were chartered between 1830 and 1860. A continuing shortage of teachers in the state led the Illinois Education Society in 1847 to begin recruiting new faculty from the East. These women teachers brought with them new ideas about women's roles; in the seminaries' atmosphere of serious study, they would nurture future suffragists, including some of the leaders of the movement.

The efforts of Frances Celeste Brard Ellis led to the founding of Illinois's first female seminary. Ellis had been teaching young women in her home. In 1833, she opened the Jacksonville Female Academy in west-central Illinois, operating from rented headquarters. Although Ellis and her two young children died in an epidemic just before the school was incorporated, it continued as an independent teaching facility until 1902, when it was absorbed by Illinois College.

In 1835, Captain Benjamin Godfrey founded Illinois's second female academy, near the town of Alton. Godfrey liked to say, "Educate a man and you educate an

MYRA BRADWELL (1831–1894)

After Myra Bradwell's 1869 application for admission to the Illinois Bar was refused, Bradwell filed suit against the bar. The appealed case eventually reached the U.S. Supreme Court, where Bradwell lost. Bradwell v. Illinois was a significant setback for women—especially married women—in its opinion that woman's proper place was the domestic sphere. Bradwell created an outlet for her knowledge of law, however, when she founded *Chicago Legal News*, a highly respected journal that gave considerable coverage to women's rights.

Myra Bradwell

Bradwell's family was involved in the abolitionist movement, which provided her, as editor of the publication, with the language and vision of emancipation. Her involvement with a network of politically active women on the U.S. Sanitary Commission during the Civil War strengthened her commitment to reform. *Chicago Legal News*, though it was primarily a resource for the legal profession, gave voice to Bradwell's interest in women's rights, temperance, and the removal of women's legal disabilities.

Bradwell's work included drafting a bill, passed in 1869, which granted women the right to their own earnings. In addition, Bradwell outlined legislation that would give a widow an interest in her husband's estate, a bill for women to hold school office, the Equal Guardianship of Children Bill, and the 1875 bill which would make women eligible for the office of notary public. In 1890, Bradwell was finally admitted to the Illinois Bar.

ELIZABETH LINDSAY DAVIS (1855–DATE UNKNOWN)

Suffragist, educator and clubwoman Elizabeth Lindsay Davis founded the Phyllis Wheatley Club of Chicago in 1896. The club later founded the Phyllis Wheatley Home, a home for single black working women. It was the largest home of its kind in Chicago and

Elizabeth Lindsay Davis

individual; educate a woman and you educate a family." He chose the name "Monticello Female Academy" in honor of Thomas Jefferson's Virginia home. When Godfrey died in 1872, the nearby town was renamed after him. The Academy taught women for another hundred years before becoming a part of the coeducational Lewis and Clark Community College.

On June 11, 1849, Anna Peck Sill founded a preparatory school for young women. The board of trustees that established Rockford Female Seminary was so impressed with Sill's teaching methods that they made her the seminary's first principal in 1851. When the school began awarding college degrees in 1882, Jane Addams was one of the first recipients. In that same decade, both Attorney Catharine Waugh McCulloch and Hull-House social worker Julia Lathrop attended the school. In 1892, the school changed its name to Rockford College, and in 1958 it began admitting men. Today, Rockford College continues a thriving coeducational program.

Another modern-day Illinois college that had its beginnings as a female seminary stands in Greenville. The school opened in 1857 as Almira College. Its founders stated in the school's second biennial report that they sought to give young women "not only an accomplished education, but one as thorough and as liberal as is enjoyed by the other sex." Despite financial difficulties over the years, the school successfully graduated many young women. In 1892 it was sold to the Free Methodist Church, and the name was changed to Greenville College. It continues today as a private, independent Christian liberal arts school.

—JANICE ROSENBERG

one of the best known in the nation. Davis also served in 1896 as an Illinois delegate to the first national conference of the National Association of Colored Women. She went on to write *The Story of the Illinois Federation of Women's Clubs, 1900–1922*, and *Lifting As They Climb: A History of the National Association of Colored Women*.

SUSAN LAWRENCE DANA

Susan Lawrence Dana

Susan Lawrence Dana (1862–1946) served as president of the Springfield Equal Suffrage Club for one year, and entertained Jane Addams and her Chicago colleagues when they came to Springfield to lobby the legislature. Three years after women won the vote, Dana was Illinois legislative chairman of the National Woman's Party and led the fight for a state equal rights law. When the bill failed in June, 1923, a bitter Dana, who had worked with legislators in the attempt to secure its passage, reported to party headquarters, "The women fared badly. I am convinced all men are liars."

KATE NEWELL DOGGETT (1827–1884)

Kate Newell Doggett had a passion for the education and intellectual betterment of women and, as a contemporary observed, she "represented and infused a higher culture in the West than any other Western woman."

She was also remembered for hosting the most lively literary salon that Chicago has ever seen. These events, held at the Doggett residence on the southwest corner of Michigan Avenue and Harmon Court (Eleventh Street), were noted for whimsy as well as intellectual fare. The programs were inevitably followed by supper and dancing, the hostess herself often dancing until four in the morning.

Kate Newell Doggett

Doggett gathered together women who met at her home to study French, German, Italian and Spanish classics. She was also an accomplished botanist, and compiled an herbal manual that was auctioned at the North–Western Sanitary Fair during the Civil War. As the only female member of the Chicago Academy of Science, she classified and arranged its valuable collection of plant specimens. She and her husband, wholesale shoe merchant William Elkanah Doggett, were supporters of the old University of Chicago located at Thirty–Fifth Street and Cottage Grove. She taught there for a year without salary to help ease the young college's financial problems.

Doggett is perhaps best known as the founder of the Fortnightly Club of Chicago. Established in 1873, the club is the city's oldest women's club still in existence. She was also a founder of Chicago's Philosophical Society and served as a member of its Social Studies Committee for a number of years.

She was a militant suffragist, speaking at a public suffrage meeting as early as 1868. She participated in a convention of the Western Female Suffrage Association in 1869, and was appointed a delegate to the Woman's Industrial Congress which met in Berlin that same year.

Elected president of the National Association for the Advancement of Women in 1878, Doggett held the position until her death in Havana, Cuba in 1884.

Your grandfather did better

than his father.

Your father did better

than his father.

Are you prepared
to carry on the tradition?

TIAA-CREF.
Proven
Solutions
To Last
a Lifetime.

Upward mobility used to be a fact of life. But life has changed. Today, more than ever, prosperity requires long range planning and innovative thinking. That's why TIAA-CREF has become the largest retirement system in the world, based on assets under management. We offer pension, investment, insurance, and personal annuity savings plans that can help you build the kind of future you've always imagined—maybe even better. To find out more, call 1 800 226-0147 for a free Personal Investing Kit, including a current CREF Prospectus. TIAA-CREF. Financial services exclusively for people in education and research.

For more complete information, including fees and expenses, please read the CREF Prospectus offered above. Read it carefully before investing.

Ensuring the future
for those who shape it.℠

CLUBWOMEN ADD THEIR STRENGTH

Long before the 1894 formation of the Illinois Federation of Women's Clubs (IFWC), women's club activity had met with difficulties in Illinois cities and towns.

Eyebrows raised at the formation of a Ladies Association in 1833 and at the thought of women's involvement in public affairs, even education. The disdain for women's "public performances" was so intense that officers of women's organizations would ask gentlemen to read their reports for them at public meetings.

The years between 1910 and 1913 were a period of growth for the IFWC as membership escalated from 30,234 to approximately 60,000. Women were testing their strength. They were banding together and learning to operate in organized groups. By the end of 1897, there were 15,000 members in 258 clubs, and membership continued to grow.

Frustration increased, however, as women's groups became more involved in seeking civic improvement and reform. There were successful endeavors, but progress was slow compared to the energy expended. The ballot seemed to be the only answer, and the clubwomen discussed at great length their need to vote. Women's clubs provided a platform for well–known suffragists. The Chicago Woman's Club, organized in 1876, counted among its leaders Jane Addams and Frances E. Willard, both of whom rallied support for suffrage among the club's members.

Women's groups were providing effective leadership in public affairs, and individuals were gaining confidence in their abilities. Convention programs featured such speakers as suffrage leaders Carrie Chapman Catt, Susan B .Anthony, Catharine Waugh McCulloch and Anna Howard Shaw. Their speeches praised the civic projects undertaken by clubwomen. But in 1909 Shaw, president of the National American Woman Suffrage Association, reminded her audience of clubwomen that "To do away with child labor and...to secure protection for women and children...you need the ballot in your hand."

Clubwomen responded. In March 1911, IFWC leaders participated in a suffrage "invasion" of the state capitol via a special Illinois Central train. The trip was led by Addams and McCulloch, and the train made stops at nine towns. Women's clubs in each location brought large crowds to listen to speeches and cheer the suffragists.

Federation leaders were among the women who spoke before both houses of the legislature and received the applause of crowds that packed the floor and galleries. There was also heavy participation by IFWC members in auto tours of the state. Not only did the clubwomen participate as speakers and members of audiences, but they opened their homes to the speakers and lent graciousness and social acceptance to the programs.

Special projects sprang up throughout the state. A typical project, sponsored by the Alton Woman's Club, was called a "school of election," designed to "teach everything pertaining to the new citizenship." One legislation chairman claimed, "The suffrage bill has given us new importance."

At an October meeting of the Woman's Club of Joliet in 1920, members heralded the coming of woman suffrage with a song ending "....When we go voting in November."

And by November, every woman could vote.

—MARY JEAN HOUDE

member of the Illinois Women's Press Association, and an appointee to the state board of prison reform during the administration of Governor Dunne. In addition, she served as president of the Illinois Equal Suffrage Association in 1897.

MARGARET ANGELA HALEY (1861–1939)

Born in Joliet, Margaret Angela Haley came to Chicago in 1882 to teach in the stockyards neighborhood. She was working at the Hendricks Elementary School in 1897 when she joined the Chicago Teachers' Federation. Haley resigned from teaching to become a business agent for the teachers' federation in 1901. She enlisted the support of the federation in many causes including the fight for woman suffrage and was a relentless watchdog for the Chicago public schools. A *Chicago Daily News* editorial called her "the embodiment of alert, informed and fearless citizenship in action."

Margaret Angela Haley

ALICE HENRY (1857–1943)

Australian–born Alice Henry came to America in 1906 and settled in Chicago, where she met Jane Addams, who sought her aid in a drive for municipal suffrage. Shortly afterward, she became secretary of the Chicago office of the National Women's Trade Union League (WTUL), writing and lecturing on its behalf. From 1910 until 1915, she served as editor of the organization's influential *Life and Labor*, a publication which served as an advocate for women and the labor movement, reporting strikes as well as national and worldwide labor organizations' activities.

Henry believed the labor movement was critical to the struggle for suffrage, having observed Australian women achieve suffrage largely through the efforts of organized labor. She felt that once women, especially working women, achieved political power, they would be in a position to influence legislation and to effect a full range of reforms.

After resigning as editor of *Life and Labor*, Henry served as WTUL secretary and as director of its school, which sought to prepare women for leadership roles in the labor movement. She retired to Australia in 1933, and died there ten years later.

Alice Henry

BESSIE ABRAMOVITZ HILLMAN (1899–1970)

Nineteen–year–old Bessie Abramovitz proved that young women can exert great influence on policy. Abramovitz came to the United States from Grodno, Russia, when she was fourteen, and began working at Hart, Schaffner and Marx menswear in Chicago. She earned five cents per piece in the vest makers' sweatshop. When the wage was cut to four cents, she and four other young women went on strike. Their walkout began the Great Strike of 1910, in which 40,000 workers were involved.

Later, Abramovitz married Sidney Hillman and they moved to New York. There she helped organize the Amalgamated Clothing Workers of America and served as the group's vice president. She was one of the few women to rise to a policy–making position in a union of men and women.

JENNIE HODGERS, AKA ALBERT CASHIER (1843–1915)

Jennie Hodgers went to the polls and voted in every election. Even her friends thought she was a man. In 1862, she reported to Camp Fuller at Rockford, and,

after what must have been a very cursory physical exam, "Albert Cashier"—as she called herself—was assigned to Company G of the Ninety-Fifth Infantry. She fought in forty battles and skirmishes over a three-year period. Cashier's comrades noted that the handsome young Irishman was aloof, but they overlooked the soldier's attitude because they admired his military bearing and recklessness.

Hodgers continued life as a man after the Civil War, collecting a soldier's pension. Struck by an auto in 1910, she was admitted to the State Soldiers' and Sailors' Home in Quincy. The physician and

Jennie Hodgers, aka Albert Cashier

superintendent at the hospital agreed to keep her secret, but her true gender was finally discovered by two attendants who tried to give her a bath. She was then forced to wear a dress until her death in 1915.

JANE CURRIE BLAIKIE HOGE (1811–1890)

The Civil War found Jane Currie Blaikie Hoge as ready as any man to serve her country. In an 1865 speech, she recalled, "When the echo of the first rebel gun at Sumter fell on the nation's ear...the women of the land, with swelling hearts and uplifted eyes asked, "Lord, what wilt thou have us to do?" The marvelous

organization of the U.S. Sanitary Commission, with its various modes of heavenly activity, pointed out the way, saying, "The men must fight, the women must work—this is the way, follow me." Hoge traveled throughout the Midwest urging aid groups to donate supplies to the war effort.

As president of the Women's Educational Association, Hoge directed fundraising to establish the Evanston College for Ladies after the war. Mary Livermore said of her, "Any movement for the advancement of women received her warmest sympathy and encouragement."

Jane Currie Blaikie Hoge

MARY HARRIS JONES (1830–1930)

Born in Ireland, Mary Harris Jones came to the United States with her family when she was five years old. In 1867, Jones's husband and four children died during a

yellow fever epidemic in Memphis, Tennessee. She moved to Chicago, where in 1871 she lost everything she owned in the Great Chicago Fire. Shortly afterward, Jones set out to work with organized labor. In 1880, she began to move from one industrial center to another, visiting areas that were hardest hit by economic depression or labor problems. She organized and aided striking coal mine workers in West Virginia and Colorado. An antisuffragist, she believed women had all the power they needed, and only had to learn how to use it. She used her own power in interesting ways; unusual tactics included organizing a march of women

Mary Harris Jones

swinging mops and pounding dish pans to scare mules and disrupt work during a miners' strike and heading a twenty-two-day march by young textile workers to highlight the abuses of child labor. Those who loved her called her "Mother Jones." Those who feared her called her "the most dangerous woman in America."

MARY ANN RICHARDSON JONES (1819–1910)

Mary Ann Richardson Jones's Chicago home was a headquarters for abolitionist meetings. She and her husband, John Jones, met and organized with John Brown, Allan Pinkerton and Frederick Douglass.

An active member of the African American community throughout her lifetime, she was involved with Ida B. Wells-Barnett in organizing the first African American women's club and the National Association of Colored Women, which was founded July 21, 1896.

Mary Ann Richardson Jones

FLORENCE KELLEY (1859–1932)

Florence Kelley worked toward enactment of wage and hour laws and the elimination of child labor. In 1892, the Illinois Bureau of Labor Statistics hired her to investigate garment industry sweatshops and Governor Altgeld appointed her the first chief factory inspector.

Largely due to her influence, the Illinois legislature passed a factory act in 1893 to limit the number of hours worked by factory women, prohibit child labor, and control tenement sweatshops. Kelley continued to work for better wages and workday hours. In 1922, she demanded to know why "seals, bears...wild game in national parks...are found suitable for federal protection; but not the children of our [country] and their mothers?"

Florence Kelley

HATTIE KENDRICK (1894–1989)

As a teacher in Cairo, Hattie Kendrick noticed that black teachers were paid less than white teachers. She initiated a lawsuit, believing the only way to change the system was through the courts. An organizer of the local chapter of the NAACP, she had become known as a local champion of civil rights by the time she won this first suit in 1946.

Over the next forty years, Kendrick would sign her name to numerous lawsuits. Perhaps the most crucial of her efforts was a suit filed in 1973 that sought to declare Cairo's commission form of government unconstitutional. Under its at-large voting system, African-Americans were effectively blocked from representation in city government.

Kendrick v. Walder, dismissed by the city, went to the U.S. Court of Appeals, which remanded the trial. In 1980, the district court entered a consent decree, and the at-large voting system was abolished. Cairo was divided into five wards, two of which were predominantly African-American. In November 1980, two African-Americans were elected to the City Council.

Hattie Kendrick

MARY ASHTON RICE LIVERMORE (1820–1905)

During the Civil War, abolitionist Mary Ashton Rice Livermore worked as co–director of the Chicago Branch of the U.S. Sanitary Commission. She traveled throughout the Midwest, forming more than three thousand local civilian units to provide soldiers with food, medicine, surgical dressings, and other essentials.

Livermore had been opposed to woman suffrage prior to the war. In her 1897 autobiography, *The Story of My Life*, she noted: "During the war, and as a result of my

own observations, I became aware that a large portion of the nation's work was badly done or not done at all, because woman was not recognized as a factor in the political world." At the end of the war, she and other abolitionist women turned their efforts to the suffrage movement.

In 1869, Livermore became founding president of the Illinois Woman Suffrage Association. She wrote, "I delivered the first lecture on woman suffrage that I ever heard, and called and conducted the first woman suffrage convention I ever attended."

Mary Ashton Rice Livermore

Livermore saw the woman suffrage question as the most

MEN WHO FOUGHT FOR WOMAN SUFFRAGE

From the beginning of the suffrage movement in Illinois, women were joined in their fight by male allies. The support of male suffragists was important, especially in the early days of the movement when general public opinion was decidedly antisuffrage.

At the founding convention of the Illinois Woman Suffrage Association in Chicago in February 1869, "Able lawyers, eloquent and distinguished divines and gallant generals occupied seats upon the platform and took part in deliberations," according to *The History of Woman Suffrage*, edited by Elizabeth Cady Stanton and others. Among the "able lawyers" were two Chicago judges, James Bradwell and Charles Waite, husbands of ardent suffragists Myra Bradwell and Catherine Waite.

Galesburg minister Edward Beecher of the famous Beecher family spoke in favor of woman suffrage. He admitted that it was an experiment "to introduce the female element into legislation; but the success of the male element had thus far been such that... things could not be much worse than they are." General John L. Beveridge, who had commanded a cavalry unit at Gettysburg and who would later serve as governor of Illinois, and his wife Helen were both officers of the convention.

From that beginning, men were always counted among the members of the state suffrage association. One of the most dedicated was State Senator Miles B. Castle of Sandwich, who served more than twenty years as chairman of the executive committee. It was because many of the members were men that the 1892 annual convention voted to change the name of the organization to the Illinois Equal Suffrage Association (IESA). In 1909, male suffragists in Chicago organized the Men's Equal Suffrage League, with former State Senator Thomas C. MacMillan, "father" of the Illinois school suffrage law, as president.

MacMillan was one of many state legislators who worked for suffrage, sometimes at a cost. Representative Homer Tice, Republican from Greenview, became so unpopular when he sponsored a suffrage bill in 1911 that all of his other bills also suffered defeat. Grace Wilbur Trout, a president of the IESA, wrote, "It certainly required moral courage for an Illinois legislator to be an active suffragist at that time."

important issue of her time. "It underlies all temperance reform work," she wrote. "It means the freeing and developing of half the human race, for, through the long past, the female half of the human family has lived in a world of hindrance and repression, of disability and servitude."

ELLEN ANNETTE MARTIN (1847–1916)

Ellen Annette Martin startled three local judges when she entered the Lombard courthouse, spectacles perched on her head and hair tied in a knot, and stated, "I invoke the majesty of the law and demand that my vote be recorded."

Ellen Annette Martin

The judges stepped aside and Ellen Martin became the first woman to vote in the state of Illinois. Later that same day—April 6, 1891—she led a delegation of fourteen women to vote in this municipal election.

Educated as a lawyer at the University of Michigan, Martin had discovered a loophole in the 1869 Lombard town charter. The charter, which used the word "citizens," instead of "men," to refer to voters, was quickly changed to close the loophole. The event passed unmentioned in local newspapers.

Several Illinois governors also played important roles in the suffrage movement. One of the most openly prosuffrage was Democrat John Peter Altgeld, who served from 1893 until 1897. He appointed an unprecedented number of women to state boards and commissions, defending the appointments in his message to the Thirty-Ninth General Assembly: "While this was not good politics from either personal or party standpoint, it was believed to be eternally right, and was done solely on the ground of justice."

Democratic Governor Edward F. Dunne signed the 1913 suffrage bill into law. Dunne, an unlikely ally, held traditional views about women's roles. However, during his term as mayor of Chicago, he became, by his own admission, converted to suffrage by Margaret Haley of the Chicago Teachers' Federation. Withstanding pressure to veto the suffrage bill, he signed it, earning what Grace Wilbur Trout called, "the everlasting gratitude of every man and woman in Illinois who stands for human liberty."

Some men who had been lukewarm or opposed to suffrage before 1913 changed their minds after the bill was signed. Among them were African American political leaders in Chicago. Robert S. Abbott, publisher of the *Chicago Defender*, who had worried about the effect of woman suffrage on the home, endorsed it in editorials after 1913. Oscar DePriest courted women's votes in his successful 1915 bid to become the city's first African American alderman. After his election, DePriest told *The Crisis*, the national journal of the NAACP, that he was a suffragist and personally grateful for the work of women voters in his ward.

When Congress passed the Nineteenth Amendment,, Illinois become the first state to ratify. Many Illinois legislators had been converted to suffrage through their experience with women voters in the state. Others simply bowed to the inevitable. Republican Governor Frank C. Lowden endorsed ratification, and Republicans and Democrats alike voted overwhelmingly for the federal amendment.

Because men controlled legislative power and most avenues to that power, it was imperative that women suffragists work with them. Some male suffragists came to the movement through a shared commitment with their wives, some through the knowledge that women's votes could be important in achieving their goals. As time passed, many accepted the simple justice of woman suffrage. As their numbers swelled, men and women suffragists together became a potent political force in Illinois.

—SANDRA S. HARMON

Reminiscent of Susan B. Anthony's 1872 attempt to vote in New York, the incident in Lombard produced few, if any, immediate results. However, Martin's actions may have influenced the Thirty-Seventh General Assembly's passage of The School Election Act in June 1891. This act allowed Illinois women to vote in state and local school elections.

CATHARINE COUGER WAUGH McCULLOCH (1862-1945)

In 1886, Catharine Couger Waugh McCulloch graduated from the Union College of Law in Chicago. Encountering prejudice there against women lawyers, she set up a law practice in her hometown of Rockford instead. Encouraged by her husband Frank Hathorn McCulloch, she became involved in the woman suffrage movement. As legislative superintendent of the Illinois Equal Suffrage Association in 1890, McCulloch wrote a bill providing for woman suffrage in presidential elections and in local elections that were not constitutionally limited to male voters.

For twenty years, starting in 1893, this bill was regularly introduced in the Illinois state legislature. McCulloch traveled to Springfield annually to testify on its behalf, and finally, in 1913, the bill was enacted.

In her treatise, "The Bible on Women Voting," McCulloch wrote:

> Women should be joint guardians with their husbands of their children. They should have an equal share in family property. They should be paid equally for equal work. Every school and profession should be open to them. Divorce and inheritance should be equal. Laws should protect them from man's greed by limiting the hours of women's labor, and protect them from man's lust by punishing severely, vile assaults on women.
>
> Women under official custody should be under the control of women. Troubled childhood should be safeguarded. All these desirable reforms can come through the vote of women and such laws have passed where women vote.

When the federal suffrage amendment was adopted in 1920, McCulloch joined the new League of Women Voters. She continued to practice law and to serve as a member of the Illinois Bar Association while pursuing her study of the world's legal systems.

MARY ELIZA McDOWELL (1854-1936)

Mary Eliza McDowell

While teaching at Chicago's Hull-House kindergarten, Mary Eliza McDowell came into contact with immigrants who worked in local meat-packing plants. In 1894, as director of the new University of Chicago settlement, McDowell moved from her family's Evanston home to the meat packers' "Back of the Yards" neighborhood.

"No social climber ever desired more earnestly to be accepted by the elite than I wished to be accepted by my neighbors," McDowell wrote. Seeing the workers' unhealthy living conditions, she began a campaign to change the city's method of garbage disposal.

THE ILLINOIS COMMISSION

to celebrate

THE 75ᵀᴴ ANNIVERSARY OF THE 19ᵀᴴ AMENDMENT

To organize statewide and local programs to educate the community about the achievements of women and the importance of the vote as a step toward achieving full equality for women in all areas of our society

Mary Jo Arndt, Republican National Committee

Prudence R. Beidler, Hull–House Association

Suzanne B. Calder, League of Women Voters of Illinois

Delinda Chapman, American Association of University Women–Illinois

Susan Gillis, Women's Bar Association of Illinois

JoAnn Horowitz, ERA–Illinois

Margaret Huyck, Older Women's League (OWL)–Illinois

Rosemary Snow, OWL–Illinois

Theresa Kern, Federation of Women Contractors

Luellen Laurenti, National Organization for Women–Illinois

Georgia Lloyd, National Woman's Party

Anne Markowitch, Jane Addams Conference

Audrey Peeples, YWCA Metropolitan

Babette Peyton, Peyton Elevator Company

Alice Phillips, National Women's Political Caucus of Greater Chicago

Pat Polos, ERA–Illinois

Hedy Ratner, Women's Business Development Center

Carol Reynolds, Illinois Democratic Women

Gillian Schultz, National Association of Women Business Owners

Natalie Silverman, Hadassah

Rebecca Smith, Women's Program at Harper College

Susan Sumner Tungate, Illinois Federation of Business and Professional Women

Elizabeth Tracy, Illinois Women in Government

Laurina Uribe, Midwest Women's Center

Theresa Cummings, Illinois Federation of Professional Women

Arabel Alva Rosales, Illinois Liquor Commission

Aware that the community's basic problems were low wages and irregular employment, she helped form the National Women's Trade Union League. In speeches and campaigns at numerous women's clubs, McDowell described the experience of the working woman. In doing so, she broadened the clubwomen's awareness of larger social problems and inspired them to social activism.

AGNES NESTOR (1880–1948)

Agnes Nestor

At age seventeen, Agnes Nestor worked in a Chicago glove factory ten hours a day, six days a week. Before long, she responded to the tyrannies of the labor situation there by leading her fellow workers on a strike. Ten days on the picket line brought them a victory. Inspired, Nestor spent the rest of her life organizing women workers. She helped form the International Glove Workers Union and later served as its president. In addition, Nestor was also a vital member of the WTUL. In 1910, she helped connect the labor movement with the woman suffrage movement when she rode the Suffrage Special train to Springfield to speak in favor of a state suffrage bill.

LUCY GONZALEZ PARSONS (1852–1942)

Known as a radical, Lucy Gonzalez Parsons was a tall woman with a powerful and musical speaking voice. Of Mexican, African and Native American descent, Parsons

Lucy Gonzalez Parsons

worked in the labor movement for seventy years. In 1905 she became a founding member, with Mary Harris Jones and Elizabeth Gurly Flynn, of the Industrial Workers of the World. In 1915, she led unemployed workers on a hunger march demanding union wages instead of charity. Parsons felt that only socialism would free women from economic, political and religious constraints and allow them to be in charge of their own lives. Although she was considered dangerous by some labor leaders, many leaders in the Chicago Progressive Movement, including Jane Addams, supported her.

MARGARET DREIER ROBINS (1868–1945)

Margaret Dreier Robins joined the women's auxiliary of the Brooklyn Hospital at age nineteen, having become interested in workers' problems while comforting crippled children who had developed rheumatism from standing in water at their jobs in rubber factories. Years later in Chicago, as president of the Women's Trade Union League, Robins rallied the organization into an effective force for labor reform. Robins spoke at meetings of the National American Woman Suffrage Association, where she stressed the needs of working women by declaring, "The ballot is the power of effective protest in modern civilization." She claimed that giving women the vote was the best way to abolish sweatshops, raise wages, shorten working hours, and establish the right of workers to organize, bargain collectively, and, if necessary, strike.

THE ALPHA SUFFRAGE CLUB

The late nineteenth and early twentieth centuries were marked by the loss of voting rights for thousands of black men, an increase in violent attacks against African Americans and the escalation of southern black migration to the Midwest. African American women in Illinois recognized that the ballot offered an effective means of addressing race problems and embraced the woman suffrage movement at both state and national levels.

Although many African American women lent support to white women in organizations such as the Women's State Central Committee (WSCC), the Illinois Equal Suffrage Association (IESA), and the National American Woman Suffrage Association (NAWSA), their efforts did not spare them the consequences of Jim Crow segregation. When they found themselves locked out of membership in predominantly white female organizations or ignored when admitted, black women devised alternative methods of pursuing the ballot. They lectured, wrote essays, marched in parades and promoted black segregated suffrage clubs. The clubs educated African American women about the political process and worked to increase the number of African American officials—a viable goal as the African American population grew in the state and as more blacks congregated in the racially segregated wards of Chicago.

One such club was the Alpha Suffrage Club. Organized in January 1913 by Ida Bell Wells–Barnett and a white colleague, Belle Squire, the club educated its members about civic matters and the significance of the ballot to both black women and working class women in Chicago. Nearly two hundred women claimed membership in the organization by 1916. They honed their canvassing and administrative skills, developed a vital political network and distributed a newsletter, *The Alpha Suffrage Record*. Their first elected officers included: Ida B. Wells–Barnett, president; Mary Jackson, vice president; Viola Hill, second vice president; Vera Wesley Green, recording secretary; Sadie L. Adams, corresponding secretary; Laura Beasley, treasurer; and K. J. Bills, editor.

It was through the Alpha Suffrage Club that African American women were represented at the NAWSA–sponsored parade in the nation's capital in March 1913. The Club sent its president, Wells–Barnett, as an Illinois delegate. But, even as the sixty–five members of the state contingent prepared for the procession, the fragile coalition of African American and white suffragists was splintered by racism within the ranks.

Grace Wilbur Trout, chairperson of the state contingent, informed the Alpha Suffrage group that NAWSA advised them "to keep our delegation entirely white" because many women, especially those from the South, resented the presence of an African American woman in the Illinois delegation. Trout then suggested that Wells–Barnett join the procession at the back of the line. She refused, insisting, "The Southern women have tried to evade the question time and again...If the Illinois women do not take a stand now in this great democratic parade, then the colored women are lost." Her plea fell on deaf ears. Disappointed with her white colleagues, Wells–Barnett left the group at the parade site. White delegates, believing that she had relented and taken her place at the end of the procession, were surprised when Wells–Barnett quietly stepped out from the crowd of spectators and joined the Illinois delegation, flanked by the only white colleagues sympathetic to her cause, Belle Squire and Virginia Brooks.

After the 1920 passage of the Nineteenth Amendment granting suffrage to all women, a united African American constituency remained a political necessity. Wells–Barnett continued to encourage vigilance among black women voters. Ten years after the passage of the federal suffrage amendment, and a year before her death, she ran for the Illinois Senate as an independent candidate. Although she lost the election, she had joined the ranks of a growing number of African Americans and women seeking public office. Wells–Barnett's legacy substantially advanced the status of both blacks and women in American political life.

—WANDA A. HENDRICKS

ANNA ELIZA CANDEE SAFFORD (1837–1921)

During the Civil War, Anna Eliza Candee Safford worked for the cause of soldiers and sailors along with her sister–in–law, Mary J. Safford. She was the

Anna Eliza Candee Safford

first woman in the West to organize camp and hospital relief for the wounded at various battle sites. Federal troops called her "The Angel of Cairo." After the war, she became a physician. When the Cairo Woman's Club and Library Association was organized in 1875, Anna Safford and another sister–in–law, Isabel Lanning Candee, were founding members, with Isabel Candee as first president. In 1894, when the Illinois Federation of Women's Clubs (IFWC) was founded, the Cairo club was its oldest member. The club thrived and later became the Cairo Public Library.

HANNAH GREENEBAUM SOLOMON (1858–1942)

A self–described "confirmed women's rights–er," Chicago–born Hannah Greenbaum Solomon resolved to form the Jewish Women's Congress of the 1893 Columbian Exposition into a permanent organization. After the Exposition, the National Council of Jewish Women, whose purpose was to teach Jewish women their obligations to religion and community, was established with Solomon as its president. Solomon worked closely with Jane Addams, primarily on committees concerned with the welfare of children. As a member of the Chicago Woman's Club, she led in establishing the Cook County Juvenile Court and in the rehabilitation of the Industrial School for Girls.

GRACE WILBUR TROUT (1864–1955)

Grace Wilbur Trout was a devoted suffragist. In 1910, as president of the Chicago Political Equality League, she launched a Suffrage float in Chicago's "Sane Fourth"

Grace Wilbur Trout

Parade. She also organized Illinois's first Suffrage Automobile Tour, an idea conceived by Catharine Waugh McCulloch. Trout is best known for having led the successful Illinois state suffrage campaign of 1913. "In New York state they told us that if it were not for the action in Illinois there would not have been national suffrage," she said. In 1919, Trout was in Peoria addressing the State Convention of the Illinois Federation of Women's Clubs when she received word that the federal suffrage amendment had passed. "Wild enthusiasm prevailed among the women when they learned the news. I was literally showered with peonies from the banquet tables and the women acted as though it was a suffrage jubilee convention."

IDA B. WELLS–BARNETT (1862–1931)

Characterized variously during her lifetime as courageous, determined, forceful, fearless, fiery and militant, Ida B. Wells–Barnett was born a slave during the Civil War in Holly Springs, Mississippi. In 1882, she moved to Memphis, Tennessee, where she taught school. In 1884, an incident occurred that led to her debut as a fearless advocate for social justice. Wells had bought a first–class ticket for a railroad trip on the Chesapeake, Ohio & Southwestern Railroad. It was a common practice for railroad personnel to force blacks to sit in the smoking car. When Wells refused to submit to this policy, she was physically ejected from the train.

Ida B. Wells–Barnett

Wells sued the railroad, but, more importantly, she wrote an account of the episode for *The Living Way*, a black church weekly. The article, signed with her pen name, "Iola," received much attention and led to her election as secretary of the National Afro–American Press Convention in 1889.

In 1892, three young black Memphis businessmen were lynched. Wells wrote editorials charging that the presumed motive—the defense of southern white womanhood—was only a pretext for these lynchings. The men had been killed, she said, because their People's Grocery Company was competing successfully with white stores. Wells encouraged blacks to boycott white businesses and to stay home from their jobs as cooks, maids and chauffeurs. Conservative Memphis whites condemned Wells for her inflammatory writing. While she was at a conference in Philadelphia, they warned that if she returned, she would be hanged in the courthouse square.

Wells did not return, but moved to New York City, where for a short time she worked for *New York Age* newspaper. In 1893, Wells came to Chicago to admonish the organizers of the World's Columbian Exposition for having denied African American participation in the fair. Despite her efforts, no changes were made.

In 1895, Wells married attorney Ferdinand L. Barnett in Chicago. Over the next ten years, the couple had four children. Wells continued her speaking engagements, and was instrumental in founding the National Association of Colored Women (NACW), the National Afro–American Council (NAAC) and the National Association for the Advancement of Colored People (NAACP).

Wells also worked with white women in the suffrage and women's movements. Recognizing the need for solidarity among black women, she co–founded the Alpha Suffrage Club, the first black woman suffrage organization.

In recognition of Wells's extraordinary contribution to society, the Chicago Housing Authority opened the Ida B. Wells Housing Project in 1941, and in 1950, the city of Chicago named Wells one of twenty–five outstanding women in the city's history. The Memphis Community Relations Commission in 1987 dedicated a historical marker at the former site of the *Free Speech* newspaper offices.

FRANCES ELIZABETH CAROLINE WILLARD (1839–1898)

Frances Elizabeth Caroline Willard

While Frances Willard is best known for her leadership of the Woman's Christian Temperance Union (WCTU), her life was shaped by feminism. At age seventeen, she resented not being allowed to share with her brother in the ritual of election, a day "which was thought to be a sacred time at our house."

After graduating from the North–Western Female College in 1859, Willard became a teacher. She worked at a variety of schools, then traveled for two years in Europe. In 1871, she was named president of the Evanston College for Ladies, but resigned in 1874. That year, Willard became involved with a group of Chicago women organizing in support of temperance—the total abstinence from alcohol as well as its legal prohibition. When the women asked her to be their leader, she accepted, resolving to make temperance her life's work. In November 1874, she attended the founding convention of the National WCTU, and was chosen to serve as corresponding secretary.

In 1876, the Illinois WCTU adopted Willard's resolution to work toward "that day when mothers, and daughters of America shall have a voice in the decision by which...the rum-shop is opened or shut beside their homes." Willard led an 1879 lobbying campaign in Springfield for the right of women to vote in local referenda on the sale of liquor.

WOMEN'S WORK AT THE COLUMBIAN EXPOSITION

A world's fair that achieved an aesthetic excellence beyond that of any previous world's fair, the 1893 World's Columbian Exposition was also more impressive in size and scope. With fourteen great buildings covering more than sixty-three million square feet, the exposition, dubbed the "White City," represented fifty-one nations and hosted 27.5 million visitors. Featuring the cultural and scientific advancements of the period, the exposition hinted at the future's promise.

The Woman's Building at the 1893 World's Columbian Exposition in Chicago was designed, decorated, and managed by women. Boston native and Massachusetts Institute of Technology graduate Sophia Hayden was selected as the architect for the Woman's Building, the only 1893 Exposition structure for which a design competition was held. Constructed between the Horticultural Hall and the Bureau of Public Health, the Woman's Building resembled an Italian Renaissance villa. Boasting a triple-arched entrance and a great skylit hall flanked by corner pavilions, the two-story, 388-foot structure was surrounded by flowers.

The building was filled with exhibits detailing the accomplishments of women in every branch of industry, featuring more than sixty women's organizations. Their achievements in the arts were represented in paintings, engravings, sculpture, needlework, literature, ceramics, and architecture; other presentations celebrated women's contributions to science and health care, invention, education, and exploration. Some highlights included a mural by Mary Cassatt, an original manuscript of Jane Eyre written by Charlotte Bronte, and a copy of the 1879 law that allowed women lawyers to plead cases before the U. S. Supreme Court.

Women's issues had been championed principally by middle-class activists. The Columbian Exposition mobilized the support of prominent upper-class women like Bertha Honoré Palmer. As president of the Board of Lady Managers for the 1893 World's Columbian Exposition, Palmer was a guiding force behind the Woman's Building. She was the wife of Potter Palmer, a highly regarded Chicago businessman. As a socially conscious upper-class woman, she was careful to confine her philanthropy to relatively conservative activities. However, Palmer, who firmly believed that "ability is not a matter of sex," gained the respect of suffragists through the work she did on behalf of women, as well as through her financial contributions to institutions such as Hull-House.

Although the Woman's Building and contributions to women's causes seemed progressive, there was a distinct lack of African American representation at the Columbian Exposition. Fannie Barrier Williams took advantage of her appointment as supervisor of exhibit installations to express an unyielding commitment to the African American cause. Recognized for her eloquence, Williams gave a speech before the World's Congress of Representative Women entitled, "The Intellectual Progress of the Colored Women of the United States since the Emancipation Proclamation." The speech gained national recognition.

The 1893 World's Columbian Exposition provided a means for women to demonstrate what they could accomplish through organization, hard work, and perseverance. The Woman's Building brought well-deserved recognition to the achievements of women and provided a glimpse of the possibilities of the century to come.

—TONJE KILEN

Willard served as president of the National WCTU from 1879 until her death in 1898. Under her leadership, the WCTU changed from a prayer society dedicated to temperance to a strong women's movement promoting a broad range of other causes in addition to suffrage. Willard viewed the WCTU as a school whose purpose was to interest women in life beyond the family circle. Her goal was to encourage them to take a more active and useful part in society. Her slogan, "For God and Home and Native Land," was adopted as the motto of the National WCTU.

Over the years, Willard's leadership of this major organization, and her links to the women who led the suffrage movement, made her one of the most famous women of the nineteenth century. The speeches she made around the country drew large crowds. By 1883, her noted sense of humor and her fame as a speaker had taken her to every state in the union. Her delicate features, close-cropped hair, and small pince-nez eyeglasses were familiar to millions.

When Willard died, more than twenty thousand people came to pay their respects. In 1905, Illinois honored her with a statue which stands in the national Capitol, and in 1910, she was one of the women admitted to the New York Hall of Fame.

FANNIE BARRIER WILLIAMS (1855–1944)

As a lecturer and clubwoman, Fannie Barrier Williams supported the cause of African American women. Born in an aristocratic family in Brockport, New York, Williams was shocked when she first encountered the treatment of blacks in the South. In Chicago, she was able to convince some employers to hire qualified African American applicants for stenographic and clerical jobs from which color alone had barred them. Williams became the first black woman admitted to the Chicago Woman's Club, and this, combined with her gift for oratory, gained her a reputation as a popular speaker at church and club meetings throughout the country.

Fannie Barrier Williams

Williams helped organize the first black hospital in Chicago in 1891. At Provident Hospital, African Americans could get hospital care denied them at other hospitals. When plans for the 1893 Columbian Exposition were underway, Williams worked hard to secure some measure of recognition for African Americans. She believed that the woman's club movement could become an organizing force for black women, allowing them to improve economic, social, and political conditions in the black community.

"We hold these truths to be self evident, that all men and women are created equal."

Declaration of Independence for Women
Elizabeth Cady Stanton, First President
of National Woman Suffrage Association
Seneca Falls, New York, July 1848

ANDERSEN
CONSULTING

*Jane Addams
Hull–House
Museum.*

WOMEN'S HISTORIC SITES OF ILLINOIS

In preparing the listing on the pages that follow, we found that monuments to women often represent feminine attributes or characteristics, rather than women themselves. A majority of public statuary represents military heroes and statesmen, few of whom were women. However, Illinois boasts several fine examples of statuary representing notable women. A bronze sculpture of Mary Ann Bickerdyke cradling a soldier stands on the grounds of the Knox County Courthouse in Galesburg. In an alcove on the second floor of the State Capitol can be found a statue of Lottie Holman O'Neill, Illinois's first woman state representative. And Emma Smith stands with her husband in one of the thirteen bronze statues that comprise the Monument to Women at Nauvoo.

Homes and institutions founded by notable women abound, as do the stories associated with their preservation. We found the one-room cabin of Jennie Hodgers aka Albert Cashier in Saunemin on the brink of destruction for lack of funds to preserve it. Then, just as we were going to press, a newly appointed director of tourism in nearby Pontiac secured funds to have the house moved to Pontiac and restored. We salute this and all future efforts to identify and preserve these special places, and we invite the traveler to visit, enjoy, and support through their interest, the women's historic sites of Illinois.

CENTRAL ILLINOIS

JANE ADDAMS'S BIRTHPLACE AND GRAVE

A bronze plaque on the gatepost and another by the front door identify this two–story white frame house where Jane Addams was born, which today is a private residence. The family burial plot in the Cedarville Cemetery is 1,200 feet down the road from the house. A small stone beneath a towering shaft reads, "Jane Addams of Hull–House and The Women's International League for Peace and Freedom." Jane Addams's gravesite is open from dawn to dusk daily.

To visit the site from Freeport, take Route 26 north to Cherry Street, west to Mill Street, then north to the house and cemetery.

The Cedarville Museum, on Cherry Street, has one room dedicated to Jane Addams's memorabilia, and is open Saturdays and Sundays, 1 p.m. to 4 p.m., April through October.

JENNIE HODGERS'S GRAVE/AKA ALBERT CASHIER

At the request of her comrades, Civil War soldier Jennie Hodgers, who fought for three years in the guise of a man, was buried in her uniform with full military honors in Saunemin's Sunny Slope Cemetery, Livingston County. The marker identified her simply as "Albert D. J. Cashier." In a 1977 Memorial Day ceremony, the American Legion dedicated a new marker engraved with the additional words: "Born Jennie Hodgers in Clogher Head, Ireland."

EWING MANOR

Hazel Buck Ewing and her husband Davis Ewing built this French–inspired Channel–Norman residence in Bloomington in 1929. Hand–hewn cypress timbers and bricks from an abandoned local brewery lend the property a rustic appearance. A member of the National Woman's Party, she picketed the White House during the 1917 suffrage campaign. After the Ewings divorced in 1931, Hazel Ewing remained at the Manor. She entertained frequently in her home, and was an activist for world peace and environmental awareness.

SANDRA S. HARMON

The Manor is located at the northwest corner of Emerson Street and Towanda Avenue in Bloomington. Now called Ewing Cultural Center, it is owned by the Illinois State University Foundation. The house is not open to the public, but visitors are welcome to stroll the grounds.

Ewing Manor

FLORENCE FIFER BOHRER HOME

This red brick house in Bloomington was built in 1896 for Joseph W. Fifer, governor of Illinois from 1889 until 1893. He lived in it until his death in 1938. Fifer's political activity and the opportunity it gave his daughter Florence to meet public figures likely influenced her own political career. In November 1924, Florence Fifer Bohrer became the first woman elected to the Illinois State Senate. She also organized the Florence Fifer Bohrer Club, which would eventually form the nucleus of the McLean County League of Women Voters. Bohrer lived in her father's home with her own family from 1928 until 1956.

Florence Fifer Bohrer Home

The Florence Fifer Bohrer Home, at 909 N. McLean in Bloomington, is a private residence.

PEORIA WOMEN'S CLUB BUILDING

The Peoria Women's Club was the first women's club in the United States to be housed in its own building. Mrs. Clara Bourland organized the club in 1886 as an art league with sixteen charter members.

The club first met in rented space. In 1894, the club's three hundred members raised $7,000 to buy property at the corner of Madison and Fayette streets. The Chicago architectural firm of Jenney and Mundie designed the club building. Built of rusticated stone, it features neo–Romanesque arched windows and doorways.

Peoria Women's Club

The Peoria Women's Club stands today at its original address, 301 N. E. Madison Street in Peoria. Its preservation is actively sponsored by the Central Illinois Landmarks Foundation, and the Peoria Women's Club continues to call it home.

"SUSAN B. ANTHONY SPOKE HERE" SUFFRAGE PLAQUE

A plaque at Main and Neil streets in downtown Champaign commemorates a local suffrage event with these words: "Susan B. Anthony, 1820–1906, Anti–slavery Agitator, lectured on 'Work, Wages and the Ballot,' April 12, 1870, in Barrett Hall on this site."

SOUTHERN ILLINOIS

ANNA'S TRAIL

Hardin County settler Anna Hobbs Bixby (1808–1869) took courses in nursing, midwifery, and tooth pulling in Philadelphia. For years, she was the only health practitioner in southeastern Illinois. "Dr. Anna" discovered, through observation of local cattle and with the help of a Shawnee Indian woman, that a common pasture weed—white snakeroot—caused deadly milk sickness, which for years had caused the deaths of many local people. She counseled farmers to uproot and burn the weed. In 1966, the American Medical Association confirmed the accuracy of her discovery.

Sites dot "Anna's Trail," which runs north from Elizabethtown through the hollows of Hardin County. For information call the Anna Bixby Women's Center, a Harrisburg home for battered women, at 618/252-8389.

ANTHONY HALL

On May 27, 1911, Southern Illinois University at Carbondale appropriated $75,000 for the construction of a women's dormitory to be named after Susan B. Anthony.

The building was dedicated on October 23, 1913, and female students lived there until World War II when it was used to house Army and Air Force cadets. In 1962, Anthony Hall was converted into office space, and today it is the home of the university's central administration.

Anthony Hall

CAIRO PUBLIC LIBRARY

In 1883, "Angel of Cairo" Anna Safford presented the Cairo Public Library building to the citizens of Cairo as a memorial to her husband, A.B. Safford. The red brick library

is an outstanding example of Queen Anne architecture. In the entrance, niches hold statues of Greek goddesses, and original stained–glass windows portray classical authors. An Eastlake staircase, ceiling and wainscoting of carved walnut, oak, and gum woods highlight the interior decor.

The Cairo Public Library, located at 1609 Washington Avenue, is open Monday through Friday 10 a.m. to 5 p.m., and Saturdays from 9 a.m. until noon.

Cairo Public Library

MOTHER JONES MONUMENT

Labor agitator Mary Jones's last words were: "Lay me to rest beside my boys in Mt. Olive. Let no traitor draw breath over my grave."

A monument in the Mt. Olive Miners Cemetery commemorates the life of Mary "Mother" Jones Jones. At the time of Jones's death, Mt. Olive was the only union–owned cemetery in the United States.

The cemetery is open to the public. From U. S. Route 55, exit at Mt. Olive east. Exact directions to the cemetery are posted on a sign as you approach town.

Mother Jones Monument

NORTHERN ILLINOIS

OUILMETTE PLAQUE

Native American Archange Chevallier Ouilmette (1764–1840), daughter of a French trader and his part–Potawatomi wife, received 1,280 acres of Illinois land in 1829 as part of the Treaty of Prairie Du Chien. Her two sections of land stretched south from present–day Elmwood Avenue in Wilmette to Central Street in Evanston, and west from Lake Michigan to Fifteenth Street in Wilmette.

A plaque in Wilmette, located at Lake Street and Lake Michigan, notes the location of the cabin Ouilmette shared with her husband Antoine Ouilmette.

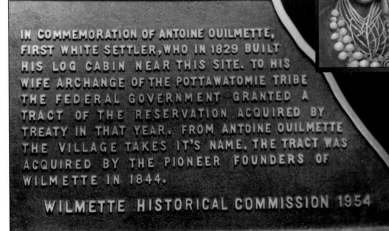

IN COMMEMORATION OF ANTOINE OUILMETTE, FIRST WHITE SETTLER, WHO IN 1829 BUILT HIS LOG CABIN NEAR THIS SITE. TO HIS WIFE ARCHANGE OF THE POTTAWATOMIE TRIBE THE FEDERAL GOVERNMENT GRANTED A TRACT OF THE RESERVATION ACQUIRED BY TREATY IN THAT YEAR. FROM ANTOINE OUILMETTE THE VILLAGE TAKES IT'S NAME. THE TRACT WAS ACQUIRED BY THE PIONEER FOUNDERS OF WILMETTE IN 1844.

WILMETTE HISTORICAL COMMISSION 1954

An artist's rendering of Archange Chevallier Ouilmette.

EARLVILLE

The first woman suffrage society in Illinois was the Earlville Suffrage Association, founded in 1855 at the home of Susan Hoxie Richardson, whose mother was Susan B. Anthony's first cousin. Richardson was inspired to start the association after hearing a speech given by A.J. Grover, editor of the *Earlville Transcript* and a male supporter of women's constitutional right to vote.

An inscription on a monument erected in 1940 in Earlville's Dodge Park reads: "Here, in 1855, was formed the Earlville Suffrage Association, with Mrs. Susan Hoxie Richardson, President, and Mrs. Octavia Grover, Secretary. The Earlville Suffrage Association was the first local Woman's Suffrage society organized in Illinois, and antedated the state–wide Illinois Equal Suffrage Association by fourteen years."

Joseph Tilton Bowen Country Club

Jane Addams and Louise de Koven Bowen looked at more than sixty sites for their country club before deciding to buy the Haines farm in Waukegan. Bowen purchased the property in 1911 and named it in memory of her husband, Joseph Tilton Bowen. Addams and Bowen reasoned that Hull–House residents and neighbors should have the kind of country club experience usually available only to wealthy people. In 1912, families began coming to the club to escape the city. They contributed what few pennies they could afford to its support. Several buildings from the original country club are still standing.

Bowen Heritage Circle is at 1911 Sheridan Road, in Waukegan. The Haines Museum and Library are open Wednesday through Friday from 10 a.m. to 2:30 p.m. and Sundays from 1 p.m. to 3 p.m.

Shurtleff Residence

This Second Empire–style house with its mansard roof and paired arched windows was built in McHenry County around the turn of the century. The original owners were Judge Edward David Shurtleff and his wife Elizabeth Sisson Shurtleff. By inviting state suffrage leaders to speak to women's groups, Elizabeth Shurtleff stimulated woman

Shurtleff Residence

suffrage sentiment in Marengo. She also encouraged her husband's support of the vote for women. In the 1913 Illinois House of Representatives—despite his leadership of the antiprohibitionists, or "wets," a group that was notorious for its opposition to woman suffrage—Judge Shurtleff championed the bill that would make Illinois the first state east of the Mississippi to grant women limited suffrage. Grace Wilbur Trout wrote: "We were especially grateful when we had secured the vote of Edward D. Shurtleff, always before opposed to suffrage."

The Shurtleff Residence, at 405 E. Washington Street in Marengo, is a private residence.

Willard House

Known as "Rest Cottage," this dwelling was built by Frances E. Willard's father in 1865. On April 9, 1900, the north half of the cottage became the headquarters for the National WCTU. In 1910, the WCTU moved into a separate administration building on

Willard House

the property. The administration building now contains the country's only temperance library. Rooms in Rest Cottage are preserved as they were in the years when Willard and her mother lived there.

Willard House is at 1730 Chicago Avenue, in Evanston. Library hours are 9:30 a.m. to 2:30 p.m., Monday through Thursday. For information, call 847/864-1397.

WESTERN ILLINOIS

MONUMENT TO MOTHER BICKERDYKE

On the grounds of the Knox County Courthouse in Galesburg is a statue of Civil War Nurse Mary Ann Bickerdyke cradling a wounded soldier in her arms. The inscription reads, "In recognition of her patriotic and heroic devotion to the boys in blue in camp, in hospital, and in the field."

FRIENDS IN COUNCIL BUILDING

On November 16, 1866, Quincy resident Sarah Atwater Denman (1808–1882) organized a society devoted to reading aloud and discussing books on philosophical and economic questions. Friends in Council was formed to spur awareness among its members and reinvigorate in them "a desire for personal, progressive growth in the direction of whatever is noble, beautiful, just and true." Still active today, the club is the oldest continuous women's study club in the United States.

The group's meetings were originally held in the Denmans' garden at Ninth and Broadway.

Monument to Mother Bickerdyke

Today, the meeting house is located on the grounds of the Historical Society of Quincy and Adams County at 425 S. 12th Street in Quincy. Visitors can view the building from the outside only.

MARY E. HOLMES (1830–1937) RESIDENCE

Galva resident Mary E. Holmes was president of the Illinois Woman Suffrage Association from 1884 until 1888, and again from 1890 until 1897. It was during her tenure that the association's name was changed to Illinois Equal Suffrage Association. She was one of the organizers of the Illinois Federation of Women's Clubs, and she and her husband D. E. Holmes were active temperance workers. After the Holmes family moved to Chicago, Galva novelist George Fitch noted the cultural void left behind. He wrote: "When [Mary Holmes] comes down from Chicago for a visit, the town fairly hums for a month. We pick up our interest in art and woman's suffrage and cheap trips to Europe and Dante's *Inferno*."

A library was set up and conducted from the bay window of Mary Holmes's residence. Here, she entertained the neighborhood children of Galva. George Fitch described a scene in the library: "Every Saturday afternoon, the muddy feet of the tough South Side kids scuffled over [her] hardwood floors, the first [such floors] west of Chicago, while their owners drew out books." The Holmes residence still stands at 708 N.W. Third Avenue in Galva, and appears much as it did at the turn of the century.

RELIEF SOCIETY MONUMENT TO WOMEN AT NAUVOO

Statue of Joseph and Emma Smith, one of thirteen in the Relief Society Monument to Women.

Within a few years of settling on the east bank of the Mississippi River, Joseph Smith, founder of the Church of Jesus Christ of the Latter–Day Saints, and his followers had established Nauvoo, the largest city in Illinois at the time. Emma Hale Smith, Joseph's wife, contributed her energies to the group's accomplishments. On March 17, 1842, she formed the Female Relief Society, which continues its work today, providing for the poor, comforting the bereaved, and caring for the sick.

Emma stood staunchly against the Mormon practice of polygamy. Yet she used her powerful position as president of the Relief Society to suppress polygamy rumors and to protect Joseph from scandal. The Mormons suffered religious persecution in Nauvoo, and after the murder of Joseph Smith in 1844 the community dispersed, many migrating to the Great Salt Basin in Utah under the leadership of Brigham Young. Emma Smith stayed behind, remaining in Nauvoo until her death in 1879.

The Relief Society Monument to Women at Nauvoo consists of thirteen bronze sculptures honoring women. Drive west from Macomb on U.S. Route 136 to Illinois Route 96, then north along the Mississippi River to Nauvoo. Admission is free.

SPRINGFIELD

DANA–THOMAS HOUSE

The Dana–Thomas house is the best preserved and most complete, as well as one of the largest and most elaborate, of Frank Lloyd Wright's "Prairie Style" houses. It was commissioned by Susan Lawrence Dana after her father, Rheuna

Dana–Thomas house

Lawrence, a wealthy businessman and former mayor of Springfield, died in 1901. She hired the young Oak Park architect rather than one of her father's associates to design the house. Today it is a state historic site administered by the Illinois Historic Preservation Agency.

The house stands at 301 E. Lawrence in Springfield, and is open for tours from 9 a.m. to 4 p.m. Wednesday through Saturday. Admission is $3 for adults and $1 for children from three to seventeen years of age. For more information, call 217/782-6776.

ILLINOIS WELCOMING THE WORLD

This statue of a woman with outstretched arms stands in the first floor rotunda of the State Capitol in Springfield. The work of Jo Daviess County sculptress Julia M. Bracken Wendt, the original plaster version was displayed in the reception room of the Illinois Building at the 1893 World's Columbian Exposition. The bronze rendition was presented to the state by the Board of Lady Managers of the Columbian Exposition, and was dedicated on May 16, 1895. Bracken, described by sculptor Lorado Taft as "the leader of women sculptors of the West," stayed in Chicago for years after the Exposition before marrying landscape painter William Wendt and moving to California, where they settled in the artists' colony at Laguna Beach.

Illinois Welcoming the World

JANE ADDAMS MURAL

In 1988, Illinois celebrated the 100th anniversary of the completion of the State Capitol Building by commissioning Illinois artists to produce four new paintings for the walls of the Capitol. One painting, "The Key," by Champaign artist Billy Morrow Jackson, commemorates Jane Addams and the Progressive Movement. A seated, young Addams comforts child laborers, and an older Addams stands holding a baby to symbolize the enlightenment of future generations. Women at the lower left carve the word "Suffrage" in stone.

LOTTIE HOLMAN O'NEILL STATUE

This bronze statue stands in an alcove on the second floor rotunda of the State Capitol. Designed and cast in bronze by sculptor Abbot Pattison, it depicts the first woman state representative as she appeared in the 1920s, early in her 38–year career in the General Assembly. The statue was unveiled on January 14, 1976.

Lottie Holman O'Neill Statue

MARGARET CROSS NORTON BUILDING

On March 23, 1995, Secretary of State George Ryan presided over a ceremony held to rename the Archives Building after the Illinois State Archives' first director, Margaret Cross Norton. A leader in a male–dominated field, she oversaw construction of the building, one of the first in the country to be designed specifically for the storage of public records. Norton started the state archive system, and served as the archives' director for thirty–five years, from 1922 to 1957. The Margaret Cross Norton Building was the first in the capitol complex to be named after a woman.

CHICAGO

THE CONGRESS HOTEL

On February 14, 1920, the National American Woman Suffrage Association (NAWSA) held its Victory Convention in the Gold Room of the Congress Hotel. With

Carrie Chapman Catt presiding, a joyous gathering of hundreds of NAWSA members formed the League of Women Voters to council soon–to–be–enfranchised women on the political process. The three–fourths majority needed to ratify the Nineteenth Amendment, however, would not be gained for another six months.

The Congress Hotel is at 520 S. Michigan Avenue in Chicago.

The Congress Hotel

FINE ARTS BUILDING

The Studebaker Brothers built this famous showplace in 1885 to house their carriage and wagon trade. In 1898 the top floor was demolished and new upper stories were added, built in terra cotta with a copper cornice. The building,

bearing the inscription "ALL PASSES, ART ALONE ENDURES," became a natural location for the studios of artists and poets, including Harriet Monroe, who founded *Poetry: A Magazine of Verse* there in 1911, and Margaret Anderson, publisher of *Little Review*. Many other women artists worked in the building, including sculptress Alice Cooper and pianist Fanny Bloomfield Zeisler.

Women's clubs also found the atmosphere welcoming. Early occupants included the Fortnightly Club, the Chicago Woman's Club, the Equal Suffrage Association, the Cook County Woman's Suffrage Party, and the Illinois Equal Suffrage Association. The Men's Equal Suffrage League was also headquartered there. Today, the building houses several movie theaters, as well as many studios and recital halls. The Fine Arts Building is located at 420 S. Michigan Avenue in Chicago.

Fine Arts Building

THE FORTNIGHTLY CLUBHOUSE

Designed by architects McKim, Mead and White, this three-story brick colonial-style house sports bay windows and attic dormers. The house was built for Bryan Lathrop, a businessman and art patron. His wife, Helen Aldis Lathrop, was a longtime member of The Fortnightly Club. The splendid Georgian mansion remained a private home until 1923. That year, The Fortnightly Club took possession of the property. In 1964, the structure was designated a Historic American Building.

The Fortnightly Clubhouse is located at 120 E. Bellevue Place in Chicago. It is not open to the public.

The Fortnightly Clubhouse

GOLDEN LADY

This twenty-four-foot-high statue is a replica of "The Republic," sculpted by Daniel Chester French of Lincoln Memorial fame. The original "lady," sixty-five feet high atop a thirty-five-foot base, looked out over the eastern end of the Grand Basin at the World's Columbian Exposition of 1893. She was made of reinforced plaster and covered in gold leaf. Her arms and head were left white for a naturalistic effect. The Greco-Roman statue symbolized the maturity of the country four hundred years after the arrival of Columbus.

The Golden Lady stands in Chicago's Jackson Park, at Hayes (63rd Street) and Richards drives (1900 East).

The Golden Lady

JANE ADDAMS HULL-HOUSE MUSEUM

The Jane Addams Hull-House Museum in Chicago is a historic landmark that commemorates the work of Jane Addams. Many influential women were involved with Hull-House, which served a multicultural, multi-ethnic neighborhood.

The nation's most influential social settlement, Hull-House was founded by Jane Addams and Ellen Gates Starr in 1889. Their work on Chicago's first settlement of this kind began in a dilapidated old mansion in a crowded immigrant neighborhood on the city's near West Side. Hull-House was an experiment in participatory democracy, a community focal point where "neighbors helped neighbors" through the exchange of resources, skills and ideas. By 1907, it had grown into a thirteen-building complex covering a city block, and had become a center for innovative educational programs, urban research, community arts, and social reform. In subsequent years Addams and her Hull-House colleagues led a national settlement house movement dedicated to improving living conditions in poor urban areas throughout the country and enacting legislative reform. This was part of a widespread movement of the 20th Century known as progressivism.

The two original buildings that make up the museum include the Hull Mansion, an Italianate structure built as a country home in 1856 and occupied by Jane Addams in 1889, and the Residents' Dining Hall, a Craftsman–style building constructed in 1905. The museum is now owned and operated by the University of Illinois at Chicago (UIC).

Jane Addams Hull–House Museum at the University of Illinois at Chicago is located at 800 S. Halsted Street in Chicago. The museum is open from 10 a.m. to 4 p.m. Monday through Friday, and from noon to 5 p.m. on Sunday, except major holidays. For more information, call 312/413-5353.

Ida B. Wells–Barnett House

This three–story Richardsonian Romanesque structure was built in 1889 of quarry–faced granite. The building's Queen Anne details include a stone gable and a corner turret covered in ornate pressed metal. The main entrance features a broad arch of Syrian design supported by paired columns topped with cushion–like capitals. The neo–Byzantine carvings on the capitals are repeated in smaller scale on single columns between the paired windows of the second and third floor. One in a row of substantially built, carefully crafted single–family homes, the Wells–Barnett house is an example of the "high–style" boulevard architecture of the 1890s. The Wells–Barnett family moved into the house in the 1920s.

ERIC FUTRAN

Ida B. Wells–Barnett House

Declared a National Historic Landmark in 1973, the house is pending designation as a Chicago Landmark. The Ida B. Wells–Barnett House, 3624 S. Martin Luther King Drive in Chicago, is a private residence.

St. James Episcopal Cathedral and Bowen Plaques

In the narthex of this cathedral in Chicago, a tablet is displayed in recognition of a gift made by Hull–House patron Louise de Koven Bowen on November 20, 1904. That contribution, which freed the parish from debt, was made in memory of her mother, Helen Hadduck de Koven. Plaques recognizing other gifts made to the parish by Bowen commemorate her father, John de Koven, and her husband, Joseph T. Bowen, longtime vestryman and warden at St. James.

St. James's interior was restored in 1985. Its elaborate system of stenciled ornament, designed by Edward Neville Stint in 1888, distinguishes it as one of the nation's finest Victorian ecclesiastical interiors. The exterior wall survived the Chicago Fire of 1871, and the tower still bears the scars of that conflagration.

The Cathedral stands at the southwest corner of Wabash Avenue and Huron Street in Chicago. It is open Monday through Friday 11 a.m. to 1 p.m. For tour information, call 312/787-7360.

QUINN CHAPEL

Chicago's oldest African American church, Quinn Chapel (African Episcopal Methodist), supported abolitionist and Underground Railroad activity. Formed in 1847, it was named after William Paul Quinn, a prominent African Methodist Episcopal bishop. In recalling the first time Susan B. Anthony spoke in Chicago, former Illinois Woman Suffrage Association president Mary E. Holmes said in 1913, "None but a colored church called Quinn's Chapel would open its doors to a woman speaker." A convention of the National Association of Colored Women's Clubs was held at the Chapel from August 14 to August 17, 1899, inspiring local clubs to form the Illinois Federation of Colored Women's Clubs.

Quinn Chapel is at 2401 S. Wabash Avenue in Chicago. For tour information, call 312/791-1846.

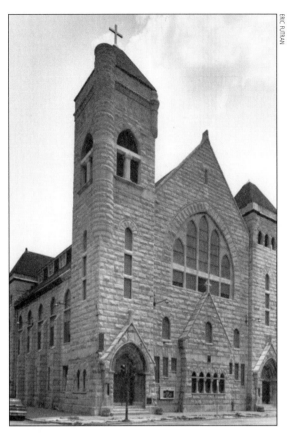

Quinn Chapel

YWCA (HARRIET HAMMOND McCORMICK MEMORIAL RESIDENCE)

Beginning in 1877, the Young Women's Christian Association (YWCA) offered young working women inexpensive places to live in the city of Chicago. The largest YWCA residence, the Harriet Hammond McCormick Memorial Residence, was dedicated in December, 1929 as a gift of Cyrus B. McCormick. Located at 1001 N. Dearborn, the building is now the Scholl College of Podiatric Medicine.

The YWCA Harris Community and Recreation Center at 6200 S. Drexel Avenue was dedicated in March 1970. Named for the family that founded Chicago's Harris Bank, it was the first new structure built by the YWCA in Chicago since the McCormick Residence. The Harris Center is the only complete program facility that the YWCA of Metropolitan Chicago operates today.

Scholl College of Podiatric Medicine (formerly the Harriet Hammond McCormick Memorial Residence)